A TRUE STORY

FAROOQ A. SHAH

Copyright © 2017 by Farooq A. Shah

All rights reserved. No portion of this book may be reproduced, stored in a retrieval system, or transmitted in any form or by any means—electronic, mechanical, photocopy, recording, scanning, or other—except for brief quotations in critical reviews or articles, without the prior written permission of the publisher or author.

This novel is based on a true story. Names, characters, places, and incidents may have been changed and are either products of the author's imagination or used fictitiously.

www.hcpbookpublishing.com

Shah, Farooq A.

ISBN: 978-0-9994025-2-8 (paperback)

           978-0-9994025-3-5 (eBook)

Printed in the United States of America.

Acknowledgments

I would like to give special thanks to those who have always believed in me and my progression: my stepfathers, Bob Campbell, Joe Faraci, Grant Garcia, Rudy Herrera, and Rich Rosenberg

To my brothers: James Garcia, Jimmy Batila, Alfredo Abate, Ramesh Ganesan, Tim Herrera, Rick Herrera, Scott Hannon, and Usman Shah.

To the staff at Rush Hospital and La Rabida Children's Hospital.

Special thanks to photographer Evan J. Thomas for the photograph used as my Author Pic.

Note from the Author

I have wanted to write a book since I learned to read. I would lay in my hospital bed, comics sprawled out, memorized by the feats of superheroes—Superman's strength, Wolverine's healing ability, Daredevil's fearlessness. I dreamed that I would become a superhero one day.

This story that you are about to read is one profound experience in my life, and I have used my superhero power of vulnerability and honesty to convey it best.

Please know I love you all, for love is the greatest of all superpowers.

Contents

Acknowledgments iii

Note from the Author v

Chapter One 1

Chapter Two 13

Chapter Three 25

Chapter Four 39

Chapter Five 45

Chapter Six 73

Chapter Seven 79

Chapter One

"If you break your neck, if you have nothing to eat, if your house is on fire, then you got a problem. Everything else is an inconvenience."

—Robert Fulghum

My life profoundly changed on July 1, 2011. It started off as a routine day, like any other. I remember that day like it was yesterday and couldn't forget it if I tried. I had gotten up that morning with no idea of what was to follow, no idea that this day would mark the rest of my life forever. I decided on a warm breakfast and fried up a few eggs and cooked a bit of oatmeal. A rerun of the game had been playing on the television and I turned it up to watch.

I remember the beads of water from a hot shower on my sandy skin as I got ready for the rest of my day at noon. I had used my favorite Adidas body wash and sung a beat from the radio. The hot water calmed my aching joints and shot nerves as I rinsed and tied a towel around my waist.

I remember walking over to the sink sometime later, and as I began to wash the dishes, the smell of lemony dish soap perforated the air. It was that special organic variety that my mom had made me buy the other day in the supermarket.

"It won't hurt your hands," she had said.

I remember there was a plate on the table, and I turned around slowly to retrieve it. I could never have known what would come next.

How often is one able to see what is about to come? I have spent so long wondering how I could have done things differently. If I hadn't moved when I had, if my reflexes had been better, if there had been more redundant strength in my body. Sometimes in hindsight after a disastrous action, we wish we could have done something to prevent it.

The shock was immediate. I felt my body jolt and jerk into limpness as I made my way to the floor with an expedient thud! It was too soon for my brain to comprehend what had happened. Within split seconds I fell face forward, my arms outstretched to break my fall, as my head bounced off the hardwood floor like a runaway basketball. I lay there finding it near impossible to move my upper body.

The next few vivid moments of my near-death experience have been seared into my being. Sometimes I'll see the whole thing in my nightmares and wake up to realize it had been real. I'll be standing near my sink again, my hands runny with the scent of lemon. I can't stand the scent of lemon now.

Time seemed to stop when I fell to the floor. A large impenetrable mass of horrifying pain emerged and I felt as if my head had shattered into a million pieces. Death seemed like an old friend to be welcomed with open arms, and while half of me entertained this thought, the other half fought violently to stay alive. I'm not exactly sure when unconsciousness took me but I'm glad it did. Some things are better left unfelt, at least for as long as possible. It seemed like years of writhing in pain had passed until silence descended and all the voices in my head went mute.

Matt told me about my unconscious journey to the hospital. How my head had hung low like I was having a painful dream that wouldn't let me wake up. The ambulance drivers handled me delicately like a piece of fine china, afraid I would shatter and they would lose me forever. If I had I been awake, I would have wondered how often people you barely know show such concern. They laid me into the ambulance with fear, reverence, and care as if I was perhaps already dead but they sincerely hoped that was not the case.

I do not remember the way to the hospital, but I try to put myself in the shoes of one of the men looking at me lying on their little bed. I sometimes try to make out what that man had going through his head. Whether he felt pity at someone so afflicted or merely the indifference that his job inculcates. He would have lifted me gently yet firmly and rushed me through the emergency doors of the hospital, and the onlookers would have gasped and then plunged themselves into action. I imagine an aura of trying to look important and useful without having any idea of what had happened.

Soon I was aware of the blood slithering down my face, leaving a striking trail in its path. I tasted its bitter saltiness, and I noticed the floor emanating coolness and letting the light play and break into shards on its surface. I was jolted to a place of complete darkness. Where was I? I had this feeling I should be afraid, but for some reason, I wasn't at all.

Whatever this place was, it was dark, like a bottomless pit that had no beginning or end. It was so truly dark that it seemed light would be swallowed here, yet somehow, I wasn't bothered by the dark at all, and felt at peace.

"I realize I am not feeling any pain! Is this what healing feels like? Oh, my God, I feel incredible! I'm so free and airy. Why am I not feeling any more pain in my body? Where has it all gone? Hey, why does it seem like my surroundings are moving away from me? But I'm not scared! Why am I not afraid? Where has my fear gone? Oh wow, I can't find the fear anymore! Is this what normal feels like? Is this what death feels like? I can't believe it; it's like a sudden wave of comfort wrapped my body in a security blanket and all the pain stopped. I'm pain-free. I can't even remember the last time I felt no pain. It's so still and so quiet here, wherever I am; it's peacefully deafening," I thought to myself.

"I'm floating in the warm darkness, pain-free. The night starts to blur like paint smearing, and it merges into the light, the edges blurring and giving way to my memories and I can see my life as a whole, no longer segmented by experiences. I'm sliding through time ...

I'm in kindergarten playing with a shiny, red toy truck in the confines beneath my desk. While all the rest of the kids sit on the carpet ready for story-time, I'm in time-out again. The slideshow continues and that moment dissipates into one where I'm standing in front of my locker in first grade asking for help with tying my shoes and my friends joke that I must be so dumb that I don't know how.

The moment shifts to the feeling of fresh, crisp, white hospital sheets on my hot, feverish skin. I remember falling in the backyard as a baby. The moments of my life come quickly in a succession of flashes. I am overwhelmed by the sense of connection to each experience, and I see something new. I am aware now of how I had defined each of those moments and what that meant to me... to my love, to my fear, to my life.

I see my sweet mother, her face stained with tears of worry, on the old murky, pink recliner near my bedside, tossing and turning to get comfortable. I see all the people that have loved me: from friends to people I do not know like doctors and nurses. The connections all come together to represent one overwhelming thought that each connection, each event was done for my betterment, that everything that happened in my life was done to teach me, to nurture me, to push me to become the person I was meant to be. Suddenly, the darkness of my suffering, the anger, the hurt that I carried with me for all of these years dissipates and I realized one thing above everything else—I was loved, and I am loveable.

For some reason, I don't feel the anguish in these memories that I know was there when I lived through these experiences. I feel peaceful and calm as I look at them. I feel incredible! I'm so free, so light! I feel like I can run! I'm healed. How am I not feeling any more pain in my body? Where has it all gone? Why am I not scared? Where has my fear gone? Oh wow, I can't find the fear anymore! Hey, why does it seem like my surroundings are becoming distant? But I'm not scared! All of the events, all of the people in my life line up in perfect harmony here in the dark.

Another wave of warmth washes over me, All the hurt, all the love, it's all here for me. In this darkness, I can see the connection. I lie there in a sobering peace, like a cool breeze. Eyes closed, arms folded in white on a white table with a warm, bright spotlight that blends with the shadows.

The images sequentially float and come together like a wormhole, one after the other. Every pain, every disappointment, and every wrong appearing like a magnificent oil painting coming together before me, for me. Suddenly I am a weeping little boy, emotional and in pain, hanging on to my mother. I'm being carried over her shoulder across the lawn, the smell of summer lemonade and linen blowing in the breeze. The wormhole slideshow flashes and suddenly I'm standing in front of the lockers of my elementary school, on the waxed, bleach-scented tiles, asking another first grader to help me tie my shoes. He pushes me off until he ultimately concedes to my prodding. The images continue, and down the wormhole I go.

Letting go of the pictures in my head has long been an ongoing struggle since they are not all the same. Some can instill such a profound sense of peace within me that I know there is peace, there is joy, and there is beauty. There is happiness for me. On the other hand, some can plunge me into the abyss and I can shine no more.

The flashes I felt in the hospital played in my head like a drive-in movie and were so bright they were blinding. As I was drawn into them even more, I saw clearly that all of these times, each moment, whether I deemed it positive or negative, didn't matter. Every one of them had been a gift. These precious gifts were given to me to make me who I am. Goodbye to the separation. Could this be the love I had longed for? The love I needed to stay alive? I then had a sense of being encompassed by pure, unconditional love.

I didn't have to do anything or behave a certain way to deserve it. This love was for me, no matter what, no matter any past wrongdoings. This was pure love, light, and forgiveness. I felt thoroughly bathed and renewed in this energy, and it made me feel as though I finally belonged, as though I'd arrived after all those years of struggle, pain, hurt and fear. I had finally come home.

What's that? I see another flash, but it's still dark somehow. It's her. Coming closer. I start to understand now who and what she is.

When I close my eyes, even today, I can still see her. I can feel her deep, profound presence. My goodbye girl. Her hair the color of summer wheat, eyes that change from blue to green, and a smile that hides the tears she's cried. She lives in a world that's always changing and letting more people in. New people, new surroundings.

She knows me. She knows everything. She can see what I want; she knows how all that I long for slips through my fingers. She knows I would die to have somewhere to belong and to have a love that stays. She hauntingly, knowingly, looks right through my eyes. She knows. She'll always be my goodbye girl. She knows it's my body that betrays me; she knows the secret even my heart won't tell me. The thing that I just can't believe could ever be true... That I could be unbroken. She knew that I didn't believe I could be complete, that I could stop wishing I were someone else.

I know she had watched over me all along, as the days passed, as my vibrant smile of childhood faded and the pain grew. I looked at her, in the darkness on that day, and I realized that I was so tired. And as I looked, I surprisingly felt an odd sense of coming home. Tired of fear, of the uncertainty, of feeling like I was never good enough for anyone to keep. Tired of straining myself to not need connection. Tired of shielding myself against rejection. Tired of moving myself between the spaces of love and relationships, dancing away the minute I saw the signs that I don't belong…Tired of feeling alone, unwanted, and uneasy. Tired of the pain. My transient existence had taken its toll.

She sees me. She sees my frail body and my numb spirit, and I can tell from the look in her eyes that she knows something I don't yet know. She knows where I'm headed. She knows my next destination. But this one is different. I look at her and see the possibility in her knowing eyes. Do I dare believe this is possible? Could this be what I've been praying for? She's the connection that I have made. She is all of the love and the loss that I have experienced; the good, bad, and ugly that I have gone through. She's here to help me say goodbye. But goodbye to what? Am I dying?

She approaches. Oh, what is that? I think to myself. It looks like a shadow coming out of the darkness. Oh, she's kneeling gently beside me. I feel the brush of her honey-colored hair, and I hear her whisper in my ear, "It's time to rise, your work is not done yet."

Suddenly my body is screaming, the peace of her aura has gone completely. I know I am in trouble, but I don't dare cry. This is the floor; this very place is where I choose not to die. I want to live. Unbelievable pain shoots through my neck. I'm awake now. I can barely open my eyes; it hurts so bad. Ugh, that's pain like I've never felt before. A wave of helplessness creeps and crawls on my skin, followed closely by a wave of regret. I have a fleeting feeling I will not be able to say goodbye to those that I love.

I couldn't move, and I couldn't feel anything below my shoulders when I fell. I lay there for what seemed like an eternity until I finally inched my way to my bedroom and pulled the sheet to reveal the treasure of my cell phone, which I used to call my friend Matt to tell him to help me get up.

I tell him I can't feel anything from the waist down and then tell him to help me up. He says, "No, Farooq, I can't." He hesitantly calls the ambulance. I tell him to stop fucking around that I just need help getting up. He, being a former EMT, knows the seriousness of the situation before I do. Oh my God, the realization comes over me— I've fallen and broken my neck.

Chapter Two

"The phoenix must burn to emerge."

— Janet Fitch

PATIENT HISTORY: The patient is a 28-year-old male who was transferred from an outside hospital after becoming a quadriplegic after a fall. C2-C6 injury with spinal cord bruising.

I could see them through my closed eyelids, I could feel that my appearance was frightening. I had a cervical collar on with tubes coming from my nostrils and arms, and my forehead was battered and bruised from the brunt of the fall. I looked more like one of the walking dead in my favorite show than like myself.

After spending a few days in the emergency ward of the hospital the ambulance had taken me to, I was transferred here because there were simply more neurologists on call. My sister and mom were distraught standing at the front of the room, and my mother was sobbing. If only they could have seen the intense irony of the situation, they might have found the whole thing mildly amusing for a while.

I wanted to comfort them but my inability to move certainly hampered my efforts. I knew my mother had a soft heart, even if it was easily misled at the best of times. Tears poured down her little, wrinkled face and she sniffed, holding up a soggy paper napkin in her fist. My sister took turns comforting her and crying herself. The whole scene seemed like something out of a soap opera.

Before I knew it, I was asleep, as the morphine kicked in and eased my muscles. I always liked going to sleep and rarely had terrible nightmares. The situation had however been reversed after the accident. As my pain gradually lessened, I drifted away to places I had never been before. I could not escape the trauma of what had happened even in my dreams. My mind played the images in close succession and I woke up abruptly, panting. My mom and sister had moved out of my room and into the corridor.

I got a peek at them through the curtains left slightly open for the 'view,' which was more than anything just stark white lighting that resembled a prison. The door had been left slightly ajar and I heard voices. It took me a few minutes to distinguish the patterns and rhythms till I could make out the concerned spikes in volume from my mother and the low, monotone which was the doctor.

I couldn't hear them properly and wanted to walk up to the curtains and peer outside, but I was in no condition to move even an inch. I struggled and strained my ears to make out what they were saying. The doctor had come in at close to 2:00 a.m. and he reflected all the tiredness that must have built up during his day.

He wasted no time in laying out the situation, and after years of handling unpleasant information, he seemed very unaffected by the nature of it. He slowly and strategically pieced the words together as if putting together a glass puzzle. "I'm very sorry," he said. "We should do surgery right away. There is a great risk involved."

I've so often been dissociative when it comes to stressful situations. Other people I imagine prefer to feel shock in its entirety and be done with it. I have always had a habit of storing it somewhere else so that it can emerge at a less than convenient time. I was trying not to listen to what the doctor was saying. *They say all kinds of things anyway.*

"It's not likely he'll walk again, but we should do surgery; there might be a chance the feeling in his legs could return." He followed the same monotonous tone as if cutting people was an everyday occurrence. It must have been for him, anyway. I felt like a third person casually observing my own misery and the fate that allegedly waited for me with its arms outstretched. In that moment, I could see the fate of a cripple catching up to me, I could also see what I would have to do to change it.

My mother seemed to have relapsed into shock and couldn't make any words leave her mouth. She stood dumbstruck as I saw her through the opening in the door and my sister took charge of the situation as she usually did.

She vehemently opposed the surgery and stated her opinion as if it was mine and told the doctor there had to be an alternative. I knew she'd do this. She was even after all these years terribly possessive about me.

"What about physical therapy?" she angrily inquired. If it had been up to her, she would have had a nervous breakdown right there in front of the doctor.

I didn't hear what the doctor said. My mom and sister reentered the room, unaware that I had heard anything at all. My sister was still trying to hold back tears and her breath was uneven. I sighed. Amid emotion, I told her to step out, but like me, she is stubborn. She didn't budge and crossed her arms over her chest and stared at me defiantly. If my neck hadn't been broken I would have gotten up and pushed her out myself. As it were, she was taking advantage of the situation.

"Step the fuck out, why don't you?" I yelled.

The dim white lights and the plain walls of my hospital room were really doing a number on me. I felt the urge to run as fast as I could even if it meant my legs would buckle beneath me. I was told this phenomenon happens to most serious injury patients, as they haven't grasped the seriousness of the condition yet. My sister remained unresponsive and there was something strange in her eyes. I couldn't think straight; I was distraught as if I was being buried alive, and she wasn't helping matters.

With a well-timed pause, they told me what needed to happen so I could walk again. I had a decision to make. The cervical laminectomy could correct my spinal column enough so I'd be able to move, but if something went wrong, I could end up in an iron lung, not only not able to walk, but not even able to breathe on my own. It was a twisted game like the ones I played as a child in which your friends would ask you if you'd rather lose an arm or a leg instead of your ability to see or breathe.

I had some medical knowledge; it's hard not to pick up when you're a frequent customer, but I was making educated guesses and then I'd shudder at the thought of the choices we had made. After all, it made no sense to talk such nonsense when we had everything in perfect working condition. I couldn't help but sob when I was left by myself. How could I decide on an action of such colossal risk? And furthermore, would I be able to live with the knowledge that I could have walked if only I'd been brave enough to give the surgery a chance?

I honestly don't know why I felt the need to call my father. Maybe it was a longing for love or acceptance from him, maybe because it was the response I was familiar with. I waited for my mom and sister to leave so I could have privacy and then picked up the sterile eggshell white phone and called him. I needed his advice. Often, we call someone hoping they give us the response we want. But people are disappointing; I had to learn that the hard way. The only person you can truly rely on is yourself.

The phone rang for a while and just when I was about to give up and hang up, he abruptly picked up the phone with a click.

"Uh, hello? Who is this?" he muttered. Leave it to him to not remember the phone number of his own son. There was so much I wanted to say. I could have started off pretending nothing had happened. I could have started off in an angry, hurt rant about why he wasn't here to see me through this horrifying period in my life. I realize now I could have done a whole lot of unpleasant things and been justified in all of them. But I was polite and dutiful as if I was a small boy again who needed his pat on my shoulder.

I perked up like a worried teenager asking for advice from someone he really held high on a pedestal. I laid my heart bare and unleashed my fears, insecurities, and the deep abiding depression that had taken hold of me. The entire time there was next to no response from my dad. There were a lot of 'huhs' and 'ohs' but no actual sentences. I felt like a telemarketer trying to sell a really boring product to someone who was just trying to figure out how to hang up the phone.

After I finished, he only said, "What is natural is natural, what is fake is fake," and hung up on me.

The starkness of his indifference stung. I wanted to sob like a small boy again, hidden under my bed. Regardless of what people say, you never stop wanting validation from your parents, especially if they don't have a history of providing it. The less they give you the more you want, even as an adult. The holes he had left in my heart, in my feeling of self, rose again like a monster. I had spent my entire life silencing the inner voices of doubt, but I had missed out on one essential thing: I was not the same person I had once been.

His words would normally have been enough to leave me in a deep depression for weeks, but I felt his words or lack thereof trickling off my back like droplets in the rain. Although I could not deny the impact it had on me, I could turn it to my advantage, and that already made me different from others. I felt a residual anger rising in me as opposed to disillusionment. My father's words had quite the opposite effect on me than the one I imagined he had intended.

At that moment, I vowed I would walk again. I'm not sure if it was for him or me, and this was the vow that would open me to a whole new life I couldn't have imagined before. Sometimes we just need a push from the negativity of others to realize our own potential. In my experience, people will always project their own failures and lack of willpower on to you.

He left me all alone, just as he had done when I was a kid and admitted to the hospital all those times. You'd think the broken neck was the catalyst in my transformation, and in many ways, it was. Onlookers described it as catastrophic, as it indeed was, but if I couldn't make it work in my favor, I don't think I would ever have gotten better.

I realized at this moment that I was the one in this situation, and the only person that I could count on to win this fight and walk again was myself. My focus was now getting through the day in one piece, continually going through the ritual of positive affirmations: "I am me" and "I am not this illness" became the identity I clung to. I had to reclaim who I was.

While my mind was poised for action, my body didn't quite respond or know what to do with the increased adrenaline pumping through my body. It seemed to be in a shut-down mode and the morphine made me want to sleep all day. The same dreams plagued my subconscious. I was running through fields; sometimes I was in a marathon. I woke up in spurts, hyperventilating, realizing where I was and what had happened.

The following night, my legs just felt like they couldn't make up their mind. Tingle, lights on, tingle, lights off—like someone had not plugged me in all the way. It was a night filled with grueling anxiety. I felt like I was drowning in doubt. I had so many questions about whether I would ever walk again, if I would ever be able to drive again, if I would ever be able to lead an independent life.

Sweet slumber came at 2:00 a.m., but it did not last long. I was up again at 5:00 a.m., awakened by a friendly face to check my vitals. She told me that the doctor would be in shortly to discuss options and get my decision about if I wanted to do neck fusion surgery or take my chances with physical therapy. She told me my spinal cord was badly bruised, which was causing my legs to feel the way that they were. I found myself thinking she had pretty hair and that she should probably be on a runway somewhere rather than here checking on patients.

Some IVs were adjusted and the purpose of each was explained, but I wasn't listening as I stared at the ceiling. Part of me was filled with willpower and the desire for action and the other part was struggling with the strain of the question, "Could I even do it?"

A few minutes later, the neurosurgeon came in. He was a slender man with newly grey hair on the sides of his head and a drawn, tired face. He stated everything very matter-of-factly, completely non-cognizant of any emotions or the gravity of the decision weighing on my shoulders. He reminded me of one of those robot cartoons I watched as a child, in which the worst possible circumstances were relayed in a mechanical way that was almost inhuman.

He stated the facts as they were, and I appreciated him for it. I could have hated him or yelled in denial but what would have been the point? He was just doing his job, without enthusiasm it seemed. If I didn't have neck fusion surgery, it would be very unlikely that I would walk again or regain use of my legs. The choice lay before me and reminded me of the blue and red pill phenomenon I had seen in the movie *The Matrix*. The choice was paramount and the skills needed to make the choice and go through with it were still so lacking.

He told me we needed to decide soon because the faster he could perform the surgery, the better the outcome would be. As he turned to briskly walk away, I felt like I was standing at the precipice of a terrifying decision.

Right before he reached the door and extended his hand to open it, I called out and said confidently, "Let's do the surgery; I want to walk again."

He turned around sharply and surprise was evident on his face. He seemed like he had never seen such enthusiasm from a patient looking at possible paralysis before. He couldn't stop a smile from forming around the edges of his lips.

"Let's go for it then," he said.

I realized I had to take my emotions and whittle them down to laser focus. I could not think about anything but moving forward. I was beginning to believe that I could make it to the other side.

Chapter Three

"There is no coming to consciousness without pain."

— Carl Jung

I have always found comfort in being in a hospital surrounded by the quiet bustle of nurses and staff along with the quiet hum of the machines. When I was growing up, I got so used to that environment that it gives me a sweet sense of home when I return. No one understood the false sense of security I felt in hospitals as a child, but one does come to terms with places that are familiar and frequently inhabited.

The day before my surgery, all manner of medical professionals visited me, still trying to gauge and accurately measure the risk as far as possible. They wanted to be sure they weren't making a grave mistake by listening to me and going through with the surgery. I barely got a moment's rest the whole day because there was always someone coming in and going out, scribbling little notes on their clipboards.

My mother, who had not left my side, occasionally complained about needing a shower or the comforts of home, but she did not move from her spot. My sister had work to get to but she checked in regularly and drank large cups of coffee from the vending machine. I wasn't well enough to eat and drink as I wanted, but she fed me slurps of yummy coffee and vanilla flavored ice cream with a plastic spoon.

My neck surgery, which was officially a cervical laminectomy with fusion and instrumentation from C2-C6, left me a bumbling mess. The doctors always tell you that you won't remember anything from the surgery because of the anesthesia, but I felt it in my bones. Long after the surgery was done, I could swear I felt prodding and poking at odd intervals. Surreal as it was I finally decided it must be psychological.

And I didn't get to fully wake up and experience the pain in one striking moment. I was placed on valium immediately afterward and that rendered me largely catatonic. I found myself wishing that a biological process existed through which I would only feel a pang of pain at once and then nothing after that. But such is life. Pain is continual and ongoing and part of growing.

I wasn't fully in my senses but my leg alternated between going numb and coming alive like a sparking wire, making me yelp out in pain. Or at least I would have if I could. I felt like I was floating in an alternate dimension in which pain was all I could feel and I craved an end to it. Above all, I craved human connection to ease the burden of being alive if indeed that is what I was.

I went into hibernation for what felt like weeks, and all of it was a blur. I had the sensation of floating and peering into my life from the outside. The shards of hope that did occur during that time happened in the wee hours of the morning. I thought of my parents often, especially experiences I had when I was young. I realized that I saw my parents under a golden light. Like most people, I believed them to be faultless, perfect beings who gave me everything I needed and would never let me down. Parents: the all-knowing, all-capable, all-powerful rulers of my childhood world and nothing they did fell into question.

It was only later that I snapped out of my wanderings and realized that my father wasn't there, and the pang of abandonment hit me square in the chest. Such a position cannot last forever. I realized I had built my life on assumptions of needing others to survive or cope.

As time went on, my mind grew along with my stature, and eventually, I began to find cracks in the armor of my illusions regarding my parents. Suddenly they could make mistakes. Suddenly they could be wrong. Suddenly they were not capable of everything. They were just human. You find that the people who raised you are just as weak and foolish as you are at times, and just as able to do good deeds in the world.

They are, you eventually realize, imperfect people working with limited information and doing the absolute best they can. You begin to see just how frail and imperfect they are. And then you truly begin to see the damage the average parent can accomplish when undertaking the gigantic task of rearing a child. When you are that child, the mistakes and failures are even more evident and you are the one that has to live with them.

For me, early life was a mixture of sadness and shame. I grew up wondering why I was different and felt as though I was trapped in a world that was not my own. That did not stop me from imagining a better life, and I kept a journal hidden in my toy trunk where I drew what I wanted. They were more than just material aspirations but rather what I wanted my self-esteem to look like if it were a person—someone who was not ashamed of who he was and who could face the challenges life threw at him without letting them destroy him.

For the longest time, those sketches and journal entries were my only glimpse into a life I wanted, and soon I grew tired of them and they gathered dust in the attic. It was painful to turn the pages and realize I still felt the same way. Like I could never feel better.

My parents seemed to be two normal additions to an average world where I was a blemish; a mishap; something that needed to be fixed. My parents were my connection to the world around me and my guide to a normal life. I trusted them. I believed in them. I followed them without question. When I was old enough to look back over my childhood, I couldn't help but shake my head. My father was no god, but at that time I didn't know what to call him.

In the wake of this extremely unfortunate event, every identity I ever had disintegrated in an instant. I was no longer dependent on anyone to instill hope in me. I knew what the nurses said as they bustled busily through the corridors. I knew they feared I was a gone case and could only get worse. I imagine everyone who did not really know me thought the same and I couldn't blame them because, for many, life is in black and white.

The life I had known no longer existed, and yet soon I would discover that a new life was destined to emerge, one that was far more meaningful and with far more substance. My old life had been built on other people's definition of who I was and should be. I used to be so attached to their version of success and allowed the outer trappings of life to define me.

After all, who can gauge the value of someone's life by what they own? To think so is indeed childish and reminds me of pompous middle-schoolers who were always telling their friends, myself included, about the new car that their dad bought. When you're younger, material things so often seem to be the most important considerations of all.

At the time, the fancy car, designer clothes, they all seemed like the answer to the unhappiness that surrounded me. If only I had them, surely I would be happy. It took me the longest time to realize that the unhappiness was inside me, ingrained like a bad memory. To remove it I would have to journey deep inside to find reserves of strength.

I used to say to myself in order to be happy I needed a vacation, a new pair of shoes, a baby. But I never was happy. There was always something else that I needed and that something else always eluded me. I had to learn to accept reality. William James the famous psychiatrist said we must take things as they are not how we would like them to be. Instead of retreating from fear, I sit with it, finding that it's never as bad as I had anticipated.

In a way, I have already died once. Anyone who has gone through great trauma will understand that it is possible for a person to despair so deeply, so painfully, that you feel there is nothing left in life. You sink to a point so low that you are no longer part of waking humanity. For me, I already felt like an alien in my home; I was dying on the inside but the accident seemed to take the very last parts of me away.

As you can imagine, I had a lot of time to think after the accident. I fretted over a life that until that moment seemed to be little more than a cruel joke. I was playing a game I could never win, and I desperately needed someone I could point a finger at. I needed someone to blame.

That person was my father.

He was the one in control. He was the one making the decisions. He was the one who had made me feel like a broken and miserable mistake. He was the one who insisted something was terribly wrong with me and insisted on trying to fix me. He treated me like I was broken. He treated me like a curse. As I laid in my bed—

images of my life passed before my eyes, forcing me to relive each moment in painfully clear detail—feelings welled inside of me more strongly than ever before.

It grew to the point of exhaustion, and I found that what I felt was my old life passing away. I was dying. All hope was gone, but mercifully not for long. I was dead just long enough to say goodbye to the old, and hello to the new. Perhaps I needed to die in order to be reborn again into someone I could be proud of and someone I could look up to.

My condition improved and I began to see the world in a new light. I was no longer a broken man. I had become a child again, fresh and new and untouched by the world. I saw myself as gaining a second opportunity to start my life over, and the sensation was exhilarating. But that wasn't all.

When I looked back at my life, it was with the innocence of a child. The pain and the discomfort were there in the memory, but it was as though the sensations were on display. It was as though the feelings that had been pulling me down were locked up in a glass case, visible but impotent. The condition allowed me to look back without the pepper of my childhood experience, and I was able to see my father in a new light.

It's hard to picture your parents as children, but it is important to give it a try. Picture them toddling around barefoot in a living room or petting a cat for the first time. Imagine your mother as a little girl in the sunshine, or your father when he had his first crush. You know what it was like because that was you at some point. That was all of us.

When I looked back, I no longer saw my father as a stern and grown man; I saw a child. I saw a boy that had grown, just as I had. I saw a scared boy with a child, trying to do his best but feeling just as helpless as I did. Compassion filled my heart, and I began to realize that he was human, just like me.

All the sadness and suffering I had felt over the years—the feeling of not being enough and the longing for more from him; the wishing he were different; the blame and the heartache—all started to slowly dissipate. The feelings melted, but they didn't go away. Instead, they became one with the peace that was with me. I looked back with a new clarity and realized my father's choices were not about me. I was not being rejected and I wasn't inadequate. I was not unlovable. I was just a scared boy, and so was he.

I believe we become equal to the people who have caused us the most pain—like my dad and I. To overcome, I needed to see him in a new light—a fair light—and in seeing beyond the darkness of my pain I could connect with myself in a new way. I stepped from the darkness and into the light where I learned to love at the deepest level.

My father was no different than me. He was just a man who became a father. I resented that he never learned to show his love to me in the way that I wanted, but was that his fault? He is, in fact, made of the same fragile material as the rest of us. At that moment, looking back at my life, I could feel a tenderness and appreciation and pure love for the little boy he once was; the little boy whose heart was full and pure and true.

Somehow this changed me.

When I awoke, I no longer blamed my father. If indeed I had followed in my life's tradition of blaming him, I would never have been able to grow out of it. The more we blame others, the less control we can exercise over our own lives. In forgiving and learning to love a difficult and less than ideal person, I was growing into a bigger and better version of myself.

I started to feel forgiveness expand through me. I could sense that I no longer needed to hold on to that anger and frustration and disappointment toward my father that had tormented me for so long. I could simply accept him for who he was and love him just because. I could love him even though he's imperfect. I could love him because he was human.

A Moment of Belief

After about a week or so, I met the rehab team who was going to help me get moving again. The doctor who led that team had a kind, Californian vibe with salt and pepper hair and gentleness in his eyes. I told him I was more than mentally prepared to take on this challenge, even if I didn't believe it a hundred percent myself. I had learned over the years to always appear far more capable than I feel.

Enthusiasm was quick to reach my nerves. The doctors had not really given me the full go-ahead but I felt myself wanting to move and wanting to put in the effort despite the pain. They were lessening my pain meds with time and I could already feel the effects as they reverberated through my body.

The next day I thought I had turned a corner and was feeling like myself again. With the sensation slowly returning to my legs, I set out to walk to the washroom by myself with a male nurse nearby. His face was turned as he scribbled quickly on a clipboard and I hoped to get some walking in while he was distracted. I didn't need people putting me down or saying things like, "You had better try to rest." I was sick of all that talk.

As soon I stood up, I could feel the heaviness of my body. Although I had actually lost weight after the surgery because of the lack of intake, I felt like I was a hundred times heavier. I couldn't help but think back to my swimming lessons when I had felt as light as air, almost as if I could have evaporated and gone out of existence altogether.

What a strange thought.

Spasms went in and out of my legs like my body couldn't make up his mind. I felt like a child who would have to undergo the grueling process of learning even the most basic reflexes all over again. It took me a minute to figure out how I would walk, like I was figuring out a complex equation in Calculus class.

Gravity had taken hold and the floor wanted to give me another hug. It felt like an alternate universe where I could be swallowed up by the floor and dissolve into nothingness. My heart started beating very loudly as I thought of my initial fall.

Perhaps it wouldn't be such a bad idea to call the nurse after all.

But before that happened, the male nurse stepped in and pushed me back on the bed. He seemed more cross with himself than me for allowing himself to lose track of his duties. His hands were rough against my sensitive skin and I felt terribly disheartened. Defeated, my ego bruised, I sat at the edge of the bed, depressed and lost in my thoughts.

The nurse sensed this and felt like he may have been too hard on me. As a way of redeeming himself, he offered hope by simply stating, "Mr. Shah, give yourself time; it will happen."

As he quietly left the room, I realized what I had to do. I had to sit with the pain; I had to stop thinking that I had to believe, and instead just believe again and again until it became habitual. Fear was my bully, and I had to reprogram my brain to think of it as my friend.

It's going to be so much fun to learn how to drive again. Yup, that'll be a treat.

Chapter Four

"Do not let your difficulties fill you with anxiety; after all, it is only in the darkest nights that stars shine more brightly."

— *Hazrat Ali Ibn Abu-Talib A.S*

I'm a stubborn, pigheaded man; once I set myself to a goal, I commit to it wholeheartedly, with reckless abandon. Before I had my neck fusion surgery, I said I was going to walk out of the hospital and nothing was going to stop me. I was going to become a bulldozer and destroy whatever was in my path. For me, it was a fight for my life, and nothing was going to beat me, including myself.

There comes a point in every man's life when he must decide whether to continue in the ways he has learned till that time or to adopt a better way of existing and of conquering. Although it had taken a massive injury to kick start the process in my brain, it had started like an avalanche. Once you remove one card of negativity and self -doubt, the entire house of cards comes tumbling down.

After I had come out of surgery, my mindset changed—maybe it was the drugs that helped provide me with the loopy clarity of my truth. I had to make peace with my pain and sit with it. This was not a fight; it was surrender to overwhelming acceptance. I've had a complicated relationship with the word "connection." I'd been sluggish and cautious to embrace it because I had always focused on just surviving through my suffering. "We," "Us," and "Community" were extraterrestrial concepts to me when it came to my comfort and relief.

Many people cannot make friends with something or someone they don't entirely understand. I understood my pain very well because it had been my constant companion for many years. The only thing necessary was for me to turn my fear and inhibitions into a feeling of friendship. After all, true friends can only help you and build you up, and they cannot destroy you.

I had to accept that I might not walk out of the hospital scot-free and that I needed help to achieve my goal. I had to accept that and then work my ass off to make it my reality. Not only accept but accept it and then let it go. Utterly let it go. The switch flipped and the next few days flew by. I had a lot to learn, and I was anxious to make progress in therapy.

Since I couldn't walk, they had me using a walker. I looked like a bent old lady but I did enjoy my first breath of fresh air in days as I took a turn in the small patch of grass outside the hospital. I looked at the clear sky and imagined I was a bird who could fly away and escape for good. Before this, I had refused the wheelchair multiple times, to the point that they had a doctor come into my room with a psychologist.

The psychologist seemed a giggly, good -humored fellow but he expressed concern on my eagerness to exert myself.

"Mr. Shah, we admire your courage and resilience, but you have to be realistic. You will need a walker and wheelchair for the rest of your life."

It's not the best feeling when people who are topmost in their profession tell you something like this. You know they are trying to tell you things as they are and not set you up for debilitating disappointment but somehow they end up doing just that. I smiled to myself and did not think it a good enough use of my time to tell them all the reasons I was the exception to the rule. It would have seemed a utopian notion and they wouldn't have believed me anyway.

I simply nodded my head and told them to leave. If they had to tell me I couldn't make it to the life I wanted, then they were as good as useless to me and I could achieve more without them.

It was a challenge! Physical therapy was grueling; my therapist, Tracy, was exactly what I needed at the time. She greatly shared my aspirations and she never said demoralizing things. Whether I would be able to walk again was anyone's guess at that point but she seemed adamant to go the distance, and I was a cooperative patient in every way.

She pushed me to my limits and past them. She believed in me and knew the hard work required to walk. We spent weeks, which turned into months, practicing on the parallel bars, with her chanting our mantra of shift your weight on one leg, leg forward, shift, leg forward. She was simplifying the motion for my brain to be able to understand and process it. We kept going around and around the inside track with my walker, learning to put pressure on my front foot to do the stairs. When she wasn't there, I made a point of learning how to evade the nurses to get in a few practice steps before they spotted me.

I continued to refuse the wheelchair for all the months I was there, as it had a symbolic value for me of helplessness and the concept of being "disabled." Being disabled I believed had nothing to do with the physical limitations that one has to put up with; it is more than anything a limiting mindset.

When I wasn't in physical therapy, I was in occupational therapy, learning how to put on my shirt and my pants, relearning how to use a knife and fork, getting in and out of a car, and napping somewhere in between to catch my breath. I took more than the recommended sessions because I didn't want to waste any time and I wanted to give my body the signal that it needed to get up and going.

One day, while I was practicing getting in and out of the car, I was having a particularly hard time and getting frustrated with it all. I told my therapist that it wasn't the way I used to do things; everything felt different, and everything was different. She, without missing a beat, profoundly said, "Everything is different and it's okay; so are you and you will find a different way."

She helped me in and out of cars for many days and soon I gained the courage to try again on my own. I wasn't entirely successful, but I was still a lot better at it than I had been before. My time in the hospital was slowly drawing to a close. I had made good friends with the nurses and doctors and they deeply appreciated my compassion for the other patients and my own humbleness of spirit.

On August 26th, I walked out of the hospital. All the nurses, male and female, lined up to say goodbye. Tracy had tears in her eyes as she saw my struggle to walk. It was a struggle, to be sure, but I was beaming with self-confidence and everyone could see it. My sister helped me into the car and thanked everyone. I remember wishing my father was there for a split second and then changed my mind quickly.

I got stronger, do you hear me? I GOT STRONGER.

Chapter Five
Growing Up Differently Abled

"I swear, from the bottom of my heart, I want to be healed. I want to be like other men, not this outcast who nobody wants."

— E.M. Forster

I wrote this poem many years ago to help me gain acceptance.

A Child's Dreams

Hope, a dream
A longing strong within my mind
To fly
Just like the kite,
To soar up high into an endless sky
Oh, I can feel it,
I'll leave this world behind me
And below.
All up here
Is clear...
...I sleep...
As the wind blows with invisible fingers
Leading my kite astray
Brushing my tears away...
Flow thru my hair, and Goodbye to all sorrow
Always hope for today and tomorrow...
Hope, a dreamsong Keep held within...
Hope is in the eye of the beholder,
The beauty's in the hope in which he holds.
A love for life should hold us all forever,
But love for all eternity's the hope...
A dream, a thing
Up high, on wings.

I spent a lot of time mentally going back and forth through my ordeal in the hospital. My therapist stayed with me through my uphill journey. We were kindred souls and she wanted me to walk almost as badly as I desired it. She was kind, nurturing and understanding like some mothers are, although mine had certainly never been that way. We practiced most days on the parallel bars and she never gave up when I faltered.

I won't lie though; the depression haunted me like an ever-present companion and it was a constant battle to get on top and leave the presence behind and get through my day. I knew deep inside I wanted to do something with my life and even if I was two steps too far away from ambition, I still wanted to experience what lay on the other side of my great struggle.

One day she suddenly asked me, "So, what do your friends say?"

Perplexed I said, "What do you mean, say what?"

She looked at me confused, and said, "Well, um, you know, about your disability, about you having arthritis since you were a kid."

The question had come out of nowhere and taken me quite by surprise that she of all people would ask it. I stood there, hands tightly gripping the bars, bewildered. I told her that my friends liked me for me and that my physical limitations had almost never come up. My personality was vibrant enough to make me a catch.

I never discussed my illness with each of them in painstaking detail because it wouldn't have changed anything nor did I ever feel particularly inclined to share my pain with others to feel better. My friends liked me and accepted me for who I am and that was that. She seemed confused but I left her and continued with my exercise without paying any attention to her expression.

That, in a nutshell, is who I am. I am a child of hate who used the transformative power of love and self-belief to change his life. I'm equal parts resilient, crazy, outspoken, reflective, and humorous; I'm the calm, and I'm the storm. I'm your best pair of ratty, worn-out sneakers with gum at the bottom and a slightly loose heel—yet neither that heel nor the gum stops you from running. In fact, they make you love those shoes even more. It gives you an extra spring in your step. When you put those sneakers on, you're telling the world that this is what a pair of old sneakers can do; this is what you can do. This is what I can do. I learned all of this on my journey... This is my journey.

Mine is a difficult journey of pain and triumph, of acceptance, of anger, fear, love and all the parts in between, and knowing that without those parts the journey would be just a little less incomplete. I was diagnosed with Systemic Juvenile Rheumatoid Arthritis

(JRA) at two years old, but I started showing symptoms when I was just about the age of one.

It's funny to me...I call it RA now because I am a wondrous adult who understands, acknowledges, and appreciates what is going on in his body. For the longest time, the RA has been a part of me, not separate from the entirety of the being. While it is painful and self -destructive, I have lived with it all these years the way one lives with an old friend they just don't know how to get rid of.

In the very beginning, my knees were always swollen and bothering me, especially when I played in the backyard with my two precocious sisters. The sun used to beat down on me, and I would run around all day and night in the backyard. I remember we had a swing set back there that I would swing on for hours, listening to the clackity -clackity -clackity -clank as I swung higher and higher, and then waiting for the climatic "launch off" where I jumped off the swing, flying in the air.

There had always been something wrong with me, something that made me different from all the other children. I remember wanting to participate in the regional races and to play tedious sports with the others like every young boy would. Each time, my body let me down. My neck breaking was just another instance in a long list of occurrences when my mind had been stronger than my body. I often felt like an alien who possessed great willpower in his head but had the brittle and fragile body of a baby.

I also remember always being hot and feverish from the RA as a child, but the thing I remember most are the countless visits to the hospital and watching the overwhelming uncertainty and fear that shrouded my parents. They, without my consent or without thought for me, envisioned that I would never live up to any enviable level of potential and would always be one step behind. Their fears were often realized in small missteps I took, and it seemed like I was always doomed to disappoint them.

I did gain a sense of gratitude for my wanton sufferings after I was discharged from the hospital because I knew they had been instrumental in getting me to the point where I was in my personal development. The pang of pain that so many childhood memories triggered was difficult to justify, but I wanted to use the pain rather than be ruled by it.

Love, they say, can bond two people for a lifetime, making them able to face all odds and overcome all foes that stand in their way. Love turns men into warriors and makes women superhuman. Love conquers all, they say. It sounds nice, and can even be true if you have lived a certain life. For the rest of us, there is another force, the opposite of love that can govern life and changes our world. What is this force, you ask? What's the opposite of love?

Ask people you know, and you will get a variety of answers, with hate as the most common response. Hate is often seen as the flip side of the same coin as love. Elie Wiesel said that "The opposite of love is not hate, but indifference." Some philosophers agree, saying that if you take away love you are left with no feeling, and hatred is just another emotion that fills the void. But for many, the competition for the most powerful force on earth is not played in the opposites, because this force stands alone in its ability to sway nations and uproot lives.

That force is fear. The transition from fear, anger, and hate to one of love, patience, and light shifted me from an individual with a physical disability and a disabled attitude to a person who believed in miracles. I took what I believed were my weaknesses, what I was so bitter about, so angry and ashamed of, and internalized them to realize that they were never weaknesses—they were always strengths, just viewed in a self-limiting, negative lens.

Fear is a bullet, ripping through this world and claiming one life after the next. Some die slowly, their hearts silently rotting around the bullet within them, while others go out in waves of tears and screams. While I will never doubt the power of love and its ability to heal all wounds and mend all hearts, nothing has been as destructive in my life as fear.

Fear is a gun and love, I discovered, was not armor. Love is not weak, and love is not without power, but in my life, love did not keep me safe. Love did not keep me from harm. Love did not give me a normal life or help me to trust. Love was not a protection; it was a treatment. The strongest power in my life—the one that moved the most hearts and destroyed the most—was fear.

Fear has won wars, decided elections, and has kept nations like North Korea isolated from the rest of the world. It's not the external, worldly fears that caused the most destruction in my life. It's avoiding eye contact with a fellow human that looks different from me. It's avoiding a neighborhood because your ex lives there and you don't want them to see you.

It's never buying a dog because you were bitten as a child. It's not being able to sleep alone in a house, or go out without a partner, or leave your home without a gun.

Fear.

It's not accepting phone calls, or taking a trip, or trying something special.

Fear.

But what happens when fear lives in your home? What happens when there is no escaping the thing that terrifies you? What happens when the thing that scares you the most is your child? I was that child. In the eyes of my parents, I was everything they dreaded. Blame it on folklore. Blame it on religion. Blame it on ignorance, or societal pressure, or on the way my parents were raised.

Blame it on the country where I was born, or the city, or the neighborhood where I grew up. Find whatever answer you like to help it make sense to you; God knows I've searched for answers. The conclusion you come to, in the end, can only ever be the same as mine: They were afraid. And I resented the hell out of them for it. If only they had taught me strength and bravery, it wouldn't have cost me so much to reach the conclusion on my own. I imagine they wanted to create ease, but they created difficulty, doubt, and pain instead. Along with a horrifying phobia that encompassed the world and everything in it.

I would like to say that I felt normal. I would like to say that I looked in the mirror and saw a regular child, just like everyone else I had ever known. I would like to say that I ran and played and laughed and built connections like they do in the movies and books. I look at a picture and don't even recognize myself. I don't know who that person is and yet I do at the same time.

I've seen the person in the mirror evolve over the years. Someone who has faced his fears and tackled them head on. Someone who has made peace with his disabilities and kept walking and moving forward. Someone who has been thrown down in the arena of life but still chosen to get back up. That's him. That's the one who has been waiting to emerge and the one waiting to be birthed. The one who has been waiting to come alive.

I would like to say that. I would like him to be real.

But I can't, not yet. I have always known that I was different. There are things about me—things I will talk about more later—that set me apart from everyone else. But more than that, even if I lied to myself and tried to say I was just like the other children in my city, my parents would never have let me believe it. They told me I was cursed. They told me there was something inside of me that was making me different; sick; unsafe. They reminded me with looks and whispers and tears that I was not like them. I came from them, but I had been corrupted.

I know you are resisting the urge to think the worst of my parents and I can certainly say that I have gone down that road and found nothing at the end of it. You will find no matter how much you blame others, there is always a part that blames you. A part that holds you and only you responsible. It was that thought among others that made me let go of the hate and the resentment.

Before you make a conclusion about my parents, I should tell you that they told me many times that the reason they felt what they did was that they loved me —the treatments and the punishments and the desperate cries for help from doctors and holy men. I was told that everything they did was for me. At the time, I tried to believe that was true.

I wanted to think that my mother and father were two people doing their best, and in a way, that was exactly what was happening. The downside was that they had no idea what to do, and were frustrated and desperate in the process. But they did it all for love, right? That was the most powerful force at work, wasn't it? At first, I tried to tell myself that, but in the end, I saw my parents under a more honest light. They were afraid they had done something wrong, and they were afraid of me.

I remember this one time they took me to a holy man called a "hakeem" and he seemed to be knowledgeable about forces that normal people like us could not deem to understand. He attempted to put me in a holy trance as he uttered verses and sentences that I did not understand. The feeling that I was not formed properly or was potentially evil was not new to me. He did his entire show and then gave me a piece of paper to put in the water I drank. Apparently, the piece of paper was the magical antidote. Needless to say, he failed.

My parents were terrified. They were so hopelessly lost, and when everything they knew failed them, they turned to old folklore and myths for answers that education could not give them. To them, as with everyone I knew, there were no more answers to be found in science. Logic and doctors and professionals had been unable to cure me. The only answers left were spiritual, and so they attempted to purge me of my sickness that way.

There was endless praying and chanting amid the fervor of their intercessions that I be cured. I had become a mere spectator of my own life, and instead of being taught acceptance, I was taught to be severely uncomfortable in my own body and to let it define me. I always wanted to be more as I read books, played with my friends, and attempted to normalize my life.

Such was my life until that fate-filled day when everything transformed—the day I broke my neck, which surprisingly was the very thing that broke me free. It was the transformative journey that within the darkness of my suffering was my light.

Fear made them so desperate for a cure that they tried anything. In the 6th grade, they even had my name changed—I used to be Omar, which most of my family still call me. I liked my name but they soon developed a deep and lasting superstitious phobia that my name was somehow a source of bad luck and was contributing to my health in a negative way.

Fear drove my parents' every move for my life. Taking me to the Middle East, because they thought I was possessed... I like to believe I'm not. Well, maybe sometimes I am especially if I don't get coffee in the morning. I actually got a huge laugh out of the alleged possession fiasco. It would have taken too much energy to stop them from their crazy actions, so I just went with it. I can safely say I was even guilty of pretending to be possessed just to see their reactions. However, it was an obsession that soon took the back seat with them and they began to look for other solutions.

I learned a lot in my earliest days about fear. Fear will make people who love you do things they normally never would, all because they don't want to see you suffer. My parents couldn't control it. They didn't even know where to begin. They just wanted it all to stop, which made the suffering worse. Both mine and theirs.

My story is a journey, one of choice, belief, acceptance, and surrender. The brokenness is my blessing. It is a story about resiliency and a change in perspective. I used to wish that if only my parents had steered me in the right direction from the beginning, so much of my suffering could have been lessened. I no longer wish for that, because I understand that I would not be who I am if it were not for them. Their faults became my strengths.

The irony of the similarity of some traits between my parents and myself is not lost on me. Maybe it's in my genes to be resilient, look at who I came from.

My parents both came over from the Middle East in the '50s, in search of a better life. My father had $20 with him and an indomitable spirit. My mother was the heart of the operation and always spoke with kind words. Both of my parents had experienced poverty that was known by only a few. Assimilation hardened my father, while my mother softened under the challenges.

They each approached things so differently—my father would plow through obstacles, completely unwavering and fearless, while my mother would approach everything with caution. Both of them had experienced such discomfort and despair in their lives, and believed that there was no way they could feel like that again in the land of opportunity, milk and honey. In many ways, their emergence in society has always been a source of inspiration for me even though the battle I faced was very different.

My father's manner was strict, abusive, and unremorseful. He would rarely smile, and he expected everyone to conform to his rules. I was afraid of him, and as a child, I made sure that I never crossed him. It goes without saying that I did want to rebel against many restrictions he had laid out, but I settled with the happy knowledge that matters would have been much worse if I was a girl.

My mother used to say, "There are some people that wake up each morning and before their feet touch the bare floor, they are ready to fight as if it is their sole purpose. That is who your father is."

In contrast, my mother was always kind to me and my siblings, and I never dreaded sharing my feelings with her. She never found a way to adequately express her grief over coming over to a strange land after leaving her country. She missed her friends and her family back home, and that sorrow was evident with the way she carried herself. She was resilient and she relied heavily on my father as her support system, no matter how verbally abusive he was.

I never liked watching my mother agree with him on everything or seek his advice for the most mundane things. I would rather she have relied on me, except she never did. The increased importance my dad was given in the house because of her submissiveness only made matters worse for my siblings and me because we never felt she was on our side. She was so scared and timid to speak her mind for fear of the backlash that she got used to holding her feelings and thoughts in.

My dad viewed my illness as a curse, and for a long time, he blamed himself and my mother, certain it was the punishment for any mistakes they may have made in the past. It puzzled me how I had become the means through which they should be punished because as disheartening to them as it was, it was infinitely more painful for me and eroding for any feeling of self-worth.

As far as I know, my father blamed me for not plowing through it. If any level of effort could have rid me of my disease I would have gladly undergone it, but I remained the way I was and only got worse over time, much to the disdain of my parents.

Disability to me was ugly. At times it has been heartbreaking, tormenting, deteriorating, deforming, and debilitating. I remember when I was about seven or eight years old, my father and I had just arrived at the University of Chicago Hospital. It was a dark, gloomy, ominous day. I remember hearing the slow tap-dancing of rain just beginning. I watched the raindrops dance across the window of the old car's door until we screeched to a halt outside the hospital.

My father came around and opened my door, as usual, my hands would not work to open the giant handle on the door —just another example of how I failed him as a son. At that time, I was going through a flare -up of RA and was in quite a bit of pain. The joints of my knuckles seemed stuck in place and filled with fluid and I could not seem to make them bend properly.

As my father rolled me across the street, he ever-so-gently bent down and whispered in my ear, "Either you start beating this illness or I will start beating it out of you."

Then he continued walking me across the street as if nothing had happened. Such was my father. I thought about what he had said quite a bit and felt envious of my friends' parents because they couldn't stop singing the praises of their sons and daughters. I felt a hole of despair forming in my chest, but that was not all that there was. There was also the anger to show him that I was more than what he had imagined. That in many ways I was stronger than him.

When I first went into remission, I was in second grade. Remission was like the shackles being taken off me. If there were a place to run I would have, and even if I wasn't allowed I would still run. "No running in the halls," the principal would yell but she couldn't stop me. The sheer freedom of movement for me was intoxicating.

Being able to run home from school, my backpack hitting my lower back, the wind blowing through my hair, I fucking loved that! I never wanted to lose the freedom of what it felt to be "normal" and free. But it wasn't long before my RA reared its hideous head. On days that I felt crummy, I convinced myself that if I could jump off the bed, there was hope for me.

My child mind found the cure! As long as I can jump off a bed, that would surely break the cycle of RA. When I went into the 3rd or 4th grade, I lived a superstition every single day, jumping off the bed and curing my RA. I remember we had a clothesline in our backyard. I pretended I was MacGyver hanging off that clothesline... I loved that.

MacGyver was like me, he could adapt to whatever circumstances he was placed in. I gained solace in the knowledge that I was a warrior against troubles far bigger than me and that I was like him; I could win. He had his pen in one pocket and a piece of bubble gum in another pocket and he could get out of whatever situation he was in. I could too. Thank God, because my remission ended. Adaptability would become my new super strength.

I remember being in 4th grade and thinking of a way to attach a fan to my crutches so that I could fly like Buzz Lightyear in the Toy Story movies. I sat in a bedroom at the edge of my bed and felt the sunlight hitting my back from the window, and I saw my crutches across the room. In my head they didn't even belong to me, but to some boy I had nothing in common with. What a welcome and pleasant thought it was.

Ignorance is bliss. Even if you get it just for a while.

I heard the fan spinning above me, but it didn't seem to be helping the fever cool down. I started to think about MacGyver again. I loved how he could pull out simple stuff and miraculously put things together in crazy ways to escape to freedom no matter what circumstance he found himself in. As I looked at these crutches, I thought, *I want to fly*.

The image of me soaring through the wide expanse of sky gripped me. No more disability, pain, or limitation. I could go wherever I wanted, be wherever I wanted. Far away from anyone who would remind me of what I could or couldn't do.

I shouted to Mom, "We have to go to the store so I can get an extension cord."

"What do you need an extension cord for?" she asked, puzzled.

I lied and told her it was for school, for a fan, and I knew she wouldn't question it too much. I duct taped everything together—the fan to my crutches, the crutches to each other, and plugged in the extension cord. I laugh even now at the spectacle concocted from a kid's imagination.

Then I found the limitation and fatal flaw in my plan. It wasn't the freedom I was looking for because the extension cord would only go so far. Disheartened, I put it in the closet next to my Jenny McCarthy poster to forever be remembered as my epic failed plan. It has taken me all this time to realize that I didn't really want to fly away from my surroundings but rather the concept that I was somehow less than others and not capable of the feats they could achieve.

I understand now that all my efforts were targeted towards making my father proud of me. I wanted him to see that I could be more than what my disability had made me and I would have killed for a drop of encouragement. He never saw me for all my reserves of strength and I never got his approval for anything. I knew he had been raised dirt poor and had to work from the ground up, but my struggles were valuable and worthy of validation in their own way. I just wish he had been able to see that.

I eventually got used to the pain of RA with all the adjustability of a young boy. It was a part of my identity. It was something that I lived with. I'm sure at this point you are wondering about a lot of things but one question in particular.

Did I ever grow out of it?

That is a trick question. At any rate, resentment, trepidation, frustration, fear, and desperation were ever present. That was the spectrum of emotions I felt growing up. Those were some of the tougher spots along my journey.

It turns out fear had me gripped just as hard as it had held my parents for all those years. As I grew older, my fear and desperation continued to drive me to research everything I could about holistic health and well-being, including Eastern healing systems.

I was seeing several specialists in natural disciplines, and I also participated in different types of healing modalities. I read as much as I could from as many sources as I could, such as Alan Watts, Rumi, Maharishi Mahesh Yogi, Jiddu Krishnamurti, Thomas Merton, Paramahansa Yogananda and Bawa Muhaiyaddeen. My nights were spent researching till I felt my head would pop. Like many youngsters, I thought the answer was on the internet or curled up inside some book, and I had yet to discover it. Little did I know the answer was inside my own self.

I practiced meditation and prayer. Five times a day I would beg God to relieve me of my hideous burden and make me like everyone else. I promised it would be the only thing I would ever ask for. Often, I felt God had abandoned me and couldn't hear my voice, but that did not stop me from my fervent devotion.

I tried hypnotherapy at a local psychologist's office and sat for what seemed like ages in front of the swinging pendulum. I became more in touch with my feelings with every visit, but my pain never subsided. I found the endless peering into my soul exhausting and fruitless, so I eventually stopped, much to the chagrin of my mother and father. The hypnotherapist had me chanting mantras and seeking myself, but perhaps I needed more than therapy to truly realize all the things I could be capable of.

I changed my thoughts with alarming regularity and changed them back again, almost certain that I was somehow manifesting my condition. The continuous meditations took a toll on me and created more stress than they abated since they had no impact on the elephant in the room: my degenerative condition.

Soon I resorted to Chinese herbal remedies. Many had to be steeped and boiled in water to be taken as tea, while others were strange colored tablets I had to take with my food at night. They smelled funny and tasted worse. I can safely say I was consistent and diligent, but there were never results worth mentioning and I felt weaker and more fragile than ever.

I remember going to the acupuncturist three times a week, literally up to my eyeballs with needles and walking away from that after two years no better than I was. In my mind, I was hopelessly broken. I clung to memories of my dad's rants in the doctor's office. Even when my dad wasn't there, I felt like I could hear his voice and it would immediately make my heartbeat go up and give me a headache.

One time in particular, I remember him shouting, "My son is helpless!"

His fist hit the table as he ranted at the doctor expecting a response. The doctor was used to patients like me with their set of angry parents. She showed barely any inclination to engage my father in an argument and shook her head in irritation.

The nurses scurried away from him as he stormed around the room in a tirade. They looked like scared animals, unsure of whether to protect me or to save their skins. He was exactly the kind of patient's family member they despised because he always made their jobs more difficult.

Pointing angrily at me, my father had yelled, "He can't do anything for himself. He's useless. He has his mama help him. He can't put on his shirt, can't put on his socks. Fix him! I want him to be NORMAL!"

Now that I am much older, I can remember these events without cringing, but for an eight -year -old, these are words which seared into his very being like a wound which can only fester over time and never heal. I imagined I was somewhere else. Anywhere but where I really was at that moment.

That day when I was eight years old, I thought I would die. I sat there on the table in the examination room, wanting to run and hide, but I was unable to move. My body hurt, my hands were knurled and knotted and throbbing, my knees wouldn't bend, and my heart broke wide open as my father raged on and on. In my childish hurt, I wanted to throw something despite the crippling fear I had of my father, but my body wouldn't aid even the most basic of actions. It was like willing a spoon to start bending.

I was terrified—terrified of the pain and the doctors, terrified of my father's anger, and most of all, I was terrified that he would never love me because I couldn't be what he wanted. I remember wanting that more than anything—the love of my father. It's what we're told, isn't it? That one needs the love of one's parents to get somewhere in life. Perhaps I had that love even if I never got to see it as most other children do. All I saw was disappointment and anger. The ugly side of life.

I watched his face redden again, and I thought he was about to start yelling even louder when suddenly I heard the kind, soothing voice of my doctor. She spoke calmly, warmly, and with such authority, I felt the whole room stop moving as we all listened to her. She had a unique presence that commands attention and submission without exerting any energy to get there.

"Your son is normal, Mr. Shah, he just has arthritis," she explained.

She spoke more, but to me, the rest of her words were just a soothing tone that further calmed the room. I watched my mother breathe for the first time in what felt like hours. The nurse moved with directness now, putting my chart back onto the hook on the wall. The other nurse gently closed the drawer as she walked calmly past it toward the door.

The doctor smiled at me and raised her arm to usher my parents into the next room while the pretty nurse with the blonde hair sat with me and told me how brave I was. The fears I felt in that doctor's office were not new for me. My father had always made it quite clear that I did not meet his standards of what a son should be.

You would think I would have gotten used to it but it took me a lot longer than I had anticipated to realize he wasn't right about me. I recall as a child when it was difficult to move or even get out of bed, I had physical and occupational therapists visit my home. During those days, my father owned a boat of a car. It was as long as it was wide and carried with it a sense of class. This car was a status symbol to him; I couldn't even get into the car by myself.

I couldn't open the doors from the outside. The door handles were the ones that you have to push up and out in a fluid motion, and my hands were not strong enough. I used to struggle with those doors until I was blue in the face. I wanted to make him proud just once but my body never assisted me.

My therapist coached me continuously on alternative ways to open the doors. I lifted with two fingers and pulled with my other hand, I pushed with my elbow and used both hands to lift, but none of her tricks ever worked. In the end, they only left me feeling defeated. I just couldn't do it.

Each time I couldn't open the stupid car door, I failed to meet my father's standards yet again, and he would rage like he'd done in the doctor's office that day. He would drag my therapist out into the middle of the driveway, and I can remember his shouting voice to this day as it resounded through the neighborhood, making my disease a source of grave embarrassment for everyone around me.

"See, he can't even open the car doors!" he yelled in indignation.

He wanted every last penny's worth that he was paying to my physiotherapist. Not only was I a terrible waste of money generally, I had become even more so after being unsuccessful at everyday tasks, despite receiving therapy. I now know that the stress behind the idea of my "recovery" may have been one of the things preventing it from happening.

To my father, the car doors were a gauge of not only her worth as a therapist, but achingly I realized it was a gauge of my worthiness too. In his eyes, I was broken, and he was living in fear that he would never be able to hold his head up high because of me. It made him lose faith.

Fear, like all other powers in the world, can be used to motivate for good or for wickedness. The fear of an automobile accident or a ticket helps to ensure drivers obey traffic laws and do not operate in a way that exceeds their abilities. The fear of seeing a loved one in misery stirs people to charitable and loving actions. The fear of death or a wasted life has resulted in millions of people eating healthier and exercising. But fear is powerful on both ends of the spectrum.

Fear has caused war, enslavement, and the abandonment of millions around the world. Fear has fueled the deaths of so many humans around the world, from homicide to genocide; it would be impossible to underestimate the number. It is what connects the soldier on the battlefield and the neighborhood watchman. It is a common factor between American television news and the Mexican drug cartels.

Chapter Six

I want to stand as close to the edge as I can without going over. Out on the edge, you see all the kinds of things you can't see from the center.

~ Kurt Vonnegut

Early morning light seeps into the cotton blanket fort that I am burrowed in. The forts I create are exquisite; I imagine them like Superman's Fortress of Solitude. My mom sits in the Pepto-Bismol colored recliner, sleeping and dreaming away. I've always been an early riser, in part due to the fear I have always had of the dark. Any creaking floorboard, rustling shutter, or random bump in the night fills me with terror.

My fear grabbed me and suffocated me. For me, it wasn't the fear of the dark but rather the chasm of emptiness, loneliness, and stillness that gripped my heart. This fear, and the grinding anxiety that it generated kept me up for many hours as a child. Even as an adult, it wasn't until I died that I grew to appreciate the solace the darkness can bring.

Darkness to me was closely related to death. My fear of darkness did not extend to me being afraid of death. Since I was a child, I had wished I was dead. It came out of necessity really; I started to believe I wasn't good enough, that I would always be in pain, and that I would grow to be a burden. I used to wish for it, to dream it, to pray for it. It consumed me. One fateful holiday winter morning, when I was around ten years old or so, I spoke with a taxicab driver who drove me home from the hospital.

He must have seen something in me because he immediately shared something deeply personal. In a thick accent, he described how he was talked off jumping off the ledge of the Golden Gate Bridge. He was just moments away from jumping; he told me that when he looked down at the water, all he saw was peace. The suffering had gone on for too long. He hated his life, his job, and his very existence was a burden. He wanted to end it.

As the wind blew into his hair and eyes, he could see the end nearing as an old friend after a lengthy separation. There was peace to be found in the jump. The last jump, he called it in his head. The last jump to end all never-ending depression. The waves in the water were terribly inviting in their blue coolness and the depths that lay underneath. He told me how he imagined his body getting stuck in the reef underwater and dissolving into nothing over time. That thought to him was terribly peaceful, like a painting he had once seen in a museum as a child of a dead girl in the water with her body caught between rocks and seaweed.

"I imagined I would end up as a similarly beautiful spectacle," he said.

He didn't jump. When I asked him why he hadn't, he replied, "The water whispered, 'Leave your darkness with me. Share your light.'"

He paused to wipe a tear out of his eye. "I decided I didn't want to end up like the girl in the painting. I wanted life. I chose life, you see."

He went into a kind of stupor as he relayed the story, almost forgetting I was there. He told me of stepping down from the ledge when he was that close to eternal freedom, because it wouldn't have been freedom. Freedom is only truly found in the fight, so he had vowed to keep fighting. He opened his eyes and continued his story, confident that I would listen to the very end.

"I got help, I went to counseling, and I found my purpose again. I found value in the transformative power that can come from the darkness by living with it, by becoming one with the darkness and the fear, and by sharing that connective experience. There are many forces in life. Some are powers we seem to hold no real control over, like affection, yet there are others like judgment and discipline that we can choose to exercise," he explained.

"These forces have no real good or evil nature as a rule. We can use affection, discipline, or even hatred like superpowers for just purposes, so long as we choose to let them motivate us to acts of justice and kindness over violence. For most people, there is a single force that rises above the rest though, as the most influential power in the world, and that force is love. People say that love makes you go beyond yourself, do things you would never normally do, and keep you committed to a belief or ideal for generations."

I didn't know what to say to the unspeakable wisdom he had imparted. I wanted to tell him about the extent of my difficulties but I didn't have the words. What he had said had resounded with something deep within my soul and even I couldn't hope to contradict it.

He parked outside my house and turned around and smiled. He assisted me out of the car delicately and I remember wishing he was my father. The gentleness he had around him made him instantly dear to me. He walked me to my door, tipped his hat, and left, looking back a few times to make sure I got in.

Chapter Seven

"Hollowness: that I understand. I'm starting to believe that there isn't anything you can do to fix it. That's what I've taken from the therapy sessions: the holes in your life are permanent. You have to grow around them, like tree roots around concrete; you mold yourself through the gaps."

— Paula Hawkins

I wrote this poem a few days after I was discharged from the hospital.

Catch

Please help me, God
I'm falling, falling
Through open air, space.
Catch me, God

I cannot move, Lord;
I am bound
To tumble and twist through the air;
There is no ground.

But if I stand,
where do I dwell?
My voice echoes
Powerful, useless
My chest heaves, for I feel I am lost.
Find me, Lord.

Sometimes I want to sink
Into the ground on which I stand
But I find it made of granite,
Not sand.

Catch me, God
I'm falling.

My mom used to say that God gave me rheumatoid arthritis so that he could make me equal to everyone else, to humble my spirit. The days immediately after I left the hospital, I felt lost, without a purpose, and yet indomitable. Breathing was the hardest part of getting out of the hospital. I felt overwhelmed by the experience of life; my brain didn't know how to process what I had been through. I was plagued with dreams of falling and overflowing with emotion like a pressure cooker without a top.

Despite all the rigorous physiotherapy I had received, I had moments when I wanted to shrivel up and never get back up. I wished I could filter out the judgment of the world and enter a void where the ugliness didn't exist. Never had I wanted to be whole so badly. For all the times I had desperately wanted my father at my side, I was actually happy he wasn't here to see me.

I became a recluse. I would spend hours staring off into space; I had no meaning and for the longest time there was nowhere that I wanted to get to in life. I didn't give a shit about anything or anyone. A paradoxical mindset followed. On one hand, I felt I had nothing to look forward to and on the other hand I was fighting for improvement in my state of living like I had never done before.

For a long time, I remember dabbling in various faiths, trying this and that to calm the tremors of my soul. It wasn't until I discovered Christianity that it all came together for me. My direction and purpose were suddenly a lot clearer than they had ever been even though they seemed like a work in progress. In the beginning, I would drive down to the local church to listen to the sermons without really grasping the effect they were having on me—I just enjoyed the tranquil environment. It was comforting for me to know there was a heavenly father. It seemed like it had been waiting for me all along and it was a truth that I just needed to realize at the right time.

I felt indestructible—I remember not looking before crossing the street; I knew that I had beaten the odds and could beat anything that came my way. My mind would race to ask myself elaborate questions like what was the purpose of this experience? What was the purpose of this pain? What was the purpose of my life until now? Where do I go from here?

I had spent all my life in survival mode, and now that mode was no longer enough. My foot had been on the gas this entire time, pushing towards my goal of what health looked like, and I became lost in that. Imagine having spent your entire life like a steam engine on its fastest route. I felt mentally and physically drained and exhausted and felt like my spirit was slowly but surely dying.

I felt the need for connection and community to feel, to dream, to be me, and to live without the constraints of just surviving. I wanted to be alive like a prisoner breathing the fresh air for the first time. I was tired of tolerating, enduring, trying. I wanted my lifelong fight to end in a victory but I wasn't ready to suffer for it anymore.

I finally decided I needed help deciphering this experience and saw a psychologist, who promptly diagnosed me with PTSD. I worked with her for the next few months, doing the emotional work I had neglected to do in the hospital while I was doing the physical work. I dealt with the fear of hurting myself again, of regrets coming from death, of gluing the pieces of my life back together with added vibrancy.

PTSD is a strange disease. As it erodes and reduces the efficiency of the mind, it impacts the body just as negatively. There are panic attacks, nausea, headaches, memory loss, and a plethora of other symptoms. I heard my psychologist say multiple times that the body is useless if one's brain is not on the right path. I was only beginning to address my depression that had spanned many years and nearly destroyed me. For the first time, I realized there were issues just as potent and destructive as my RA.

I had my sister drive me to therapy and then back again. As it began to bring about changes in my personality, which were more than welcome, I decided to reintegrate myself back into society. Gradually, my life's heart began to beat again. I got back to work, started swimming again, and met with friends again. I had an added depth and dimension to my interactions now that I had evolved from this experience, and my friends definitely sensed it.

I empathized with others easier; it was easier to be grateful to people in my life that I didn't care for. Life as a whole improved. I was still a particular and peculiar guy with RA, but this experience changed me. It made me see the power in my choices, the power in my appreciation of others, my connection to life, and how grateful I was to LIVE this life.

After years of visiting church service, I decided to be baptized so I could cement my faith. It also meant I had finally decided to carve a new, spiritually nourishing path for myself that was of my choosing and no one else's.

As a child, I had become infatuated with the sense of belonging, and that led me to a road of anger and craving perfection. I believed that by committing to perfection and gaining knowledge that somehow I would be able to compensate for my disability. More than anything, I had wanted to gain the admiration of my father, but wanting love from an abusive person is about as terrible as it sounds.

I was not the only person in this world to have craved and once worshiped external validation, but whoever that guy was, he was gone, and this new, improved person stood in his place. Someone who was no longer ashamed or terrified. I knew exactly who I was, which is why I was more confident and difficult to manipulate, even by my own lesser impulses.

I would have fought that same fight had I not hurt my neck, and it would have lasted my entire life and only ended in failure. There was no way to win. There was no way to overcome or erase who I was. No matter how hard I worked, how much I learned, or how much I tried to make other areas of my life perfect, it would not have erased who I was. It took the fall, the plunge, whatever you want to call it, to give me a new life. A life I could be proud of.

My near-death experience forced me, as the innate problem solver that I am, to step out of my old belief system, the one that said either you were perfect or you were worthless—and accept a new truth: I am me. I am lovable and worthy of connection. No more, no less. And that was fine. What I can accept, I can endure. No avoidance, just profound acceptance.

From that day going forward, I stayed ready for my first step or my last, turning each step towards the darkness into the light. It took all the energy I had left in me after all these years. The therapy I had undergone helped me uncover new reservoirs of strength that I didn't know existed within me. For all my progress, there were still times I felt like giving up. It was a bipolar feeling and like trying to balance a see-saw.

In the aftermath of my diagnosis, I struggled to fight the darkness. Despite feeling a little better physically, I found myself not wanting to get out of bed. I felt like my life was over before it had even begun. Any hopes I had of a normal life, career or even family suddenly seemed out of reach. I felt like there was no hope. I was told by many that this was to be expected in the wake of what I had suffered. I needed to be patient, they said. I felt like yelling at them and calling them out on their sheer ignorance but I was not my father, so I never said anything.

It took me a few weeks to realize I couldn't live this way. I couldn't restrict myself and treat myself like I was sick and fragile. Two weeks after my diagnosis I had made a crucial choice, one that will continue to have an impact on me for the rest of my life: I chose to fight back. I needed to remember the strength that had taken me to where I am. I needed to always remember

I was capable of such strength. And could most people say the same about themselves? I think not.

I began to drag myself out of bed in the morning. My entire body hurt, and I constantly felt sick, but I made a promise to myself that I was going to fight with everything in me. I would not let this disease define me and decide my life for me. I took the small steps first. I got up, had a nice breakfast, meditated, and prayed for a while and then pushed myself to go for a walk. It was a slow walk at first, marked with effort and strain, but soon I could build up to a considerable jog even in the colder winter months.

I was immensely proud of myself, and most of my free time was dedicated to watching nutrition and strength training videos. I was never going to be a bodybuilder, but I stood a pretty good chance of living a worthwhile and healthy life. I did sometimes hear the words of my father in my head but I pushed them out. Although I had forgiven him, I did not want to dampen the joy of my considerable recovery by inviting his opinions. I was enough for myself even if I was never going to be enough for him.

Even now, every day I have to push myself to go on. It's not easy, but some days are easier than others. With chronic disease, every single day is a battle against your own body. You constantly have to fight back and propel yourself forward. It's exhausting, and there are days when I just have to lay in bed because I don't have the energy that day, and that's OK.

The major revelation has been that I no longer hold myself to impossible standards, which are then reinforced by the people in my life. I surround myself with people that encourage me, cheer me up, and are a constant reminder that life doesn't need to be so serious all the time.

In the famous words of John Green, "Pain demands to be felt," and this rings true of physical and emotional pain. Feeling pain is part of who we are as humans, and despite how it makes us feel at the moment, it makes us stronger in the long run. I didn't know how tough I could be and how hard I could fight until I was faced with my diagnosis.

Since then, I have become my own cheerleader and my own biggest fan. I learned that above all, you must fight for yourself because you and you alone are your own strongest warrior. It's not supposed to come easy and it doesn't come naturally, but it is an acquired taste—the taste for life, survival, and reaching happiness despite your deprivations.

My disease taught me to appreciate the little things in life because when your daily life is limited, the little things become the big things. You learn to cherish every moment and celebrate your victories, no matter how small, even if it's just getting out of bed in the morning. More than anything, you learn how to love yourself. You come to appreciate your body, even when it isn't working how you want it to. You find out how to believe in yourself and push yourself to go on, even when it seems impossible.

Most of all, you learn to see the beauty of life and the wonder of the world around you, whether you are viewing it during a walk through the park or from a day spent in bed. You don't know strength until it's your only option. You don't know what it means to fully show up until you're pushed so much that it's your only choice. You don't know what it's like to be fully present and focused until you have no other option.

My sister and I took a walk in the park one day and suddenly I found her giggling.

"What's wrong with you?" I asked, laughing too.

"I'm just happy to see you like this. I never did see you like this you know," she replied.

"Like what?"

"Like a whole person who is remotely happy," she said.

Life is a trial and yet there is always another choice, isn't there? Yes. But you get to the point that the other way, the way you've been doing things, is just too painful and you've been there so many times that you want to choose differently. Sometimes you have to suffer to finally choose a different way. Old habits fall away because you just can't even handle them anymore.

These limiting thoughts flow to this day, and all I can say to them is, "No, I can't even," and keep on doing what I was doing.

I wouldn't say I'm fully there; My mindset is not that of what I imagine as a stable and high-functioning person, but I take great pride in my small victories. In finding this new addiction of gratitude, the quality of my life has significantly increased and I no longer covet the blessings of others.

I realize now that I am addicted to thinking and to over analyzing everything. My thinking is seductive, and it feels comfy and safe, but I must not give in to it. The good stuff is outside of thinking. It's all there. Right there in front of me. That's where Life is.

My purpose finds me when I start to open up to the possibilities and become aware of what lights me up. It is a matter of perception and I am slowly mastering that skill, and I learn new tricks every day. I do not get attached to any one goal but give all of them my best shot and then take what I can get. I have crushed the scarcity mindset once and for all.

A Moment of Belief

I will experience pain as long as I am alive, but I can feel it and acknowledge it and not suffer. Suffering is a choice. It has always been a choice. So that's what I do today. I just keep showing up and doing what is required and do the best I can and know that it's enough. Because it is.

I celebrate life even more now because I remember the time that I never thought I would make it out. There were so many people I wanted to say goodbye to, but I wasn't sure I'd ever see them again. But I made it out, albeit at great personal cost. And now looking back, I do not resent the heavy price tag my life has been.

For the first two weeks after my discharge from the hospital, it felt like a thought bubble followed me around like you see in the comics in the Sunday newspaper. *"Farooq Shah is a good man; he's going to make it if he can find his way to love, for that is all he really needs."* I ignored the notion then, but now it fills me to the brim. The change does not define me but rather how I rose to the challenge to make my dreams of self-belief come true.

I understand the interconnectedness of it all. I see deeper connections, and I have a deeper sense of faith, I value the connections I have in this life. The people that love me through my hardest days. My unwillingness to let go stopped my change and growth, but pain, which

I once regarded as an enemy, has now become a friend and provided me with clarity. For all is good and all is God. Bring it. I'm ready. I can go the distance and my feet are not an impediment, they are the tools that will get me there.

This skin is my skin, these bones are my home, and this truth is mine to live with, now and forever more.

Breathe.

www.ingramcontent.com/pod-product-compliance
Lightning Source LLC
Chambersburg PA
CBHW070544300426
44113CB00011B/1792